CONTEMPORARY POETRY

CONTEMPORARY POETRY OF THE NEGRO

BY ROBERT T. KERLIN

The Black Heritage Library Collection

 BOOKS FOR LIBRARIES PRESS
FREEPORT, NEW YORK
1971

First Published 1921
Reprinted 1971

Reprinted from a copy in the
Fisk University Library Negro Collection

INTERNATIONAL STANDARD BOOK NUMBER:
0-8369-8945-7

LIBRARY OF CONGRESS CATALOG CARD NUMBER:
74-37308

PRINTED IN THE UNITED STATES OF AMERICA
BY
NEW WORLD BOOK MANUFACTURING CO., INC.
HALLANDALE, FLORIDA 33009

CONTEMPORARY POETRY OF THE NEGRO

BY ROBERT T. KERLIN

A poet of our day sings, optimistically:

> I will suppose that fate is just,
> I will suppose that grief is wise,
> And I will tread what path I must
> To enter Paradise.
> —*Joseph S. Cotter, Sr.*

Another sings:

> We have fashioned laughter
> Out of tears and pain,
> But the moment after—
> Pain and tears again.
> —*Charles Bertram Johnson*

And yet another, as from a broken heart, sings sadly and sweetly:

> The dreams of the dreamer
> Are life-drops that pass
> The break in the heart
> To the soul's hour-glass.
>
> The songs of the singer
> Are tones that repeat
> The cry of the heart
> Till it ceases to beat.
> —*Georgia Douglas Johnson*

With yearning vision, yet another sings:

A FAR COUNTRY

> Beyond the cities I have seen,
> Beyond the wrack and din,
> There is a wide and fair demesne
> Where I have never been.
>
> Away from desert wastes of greed,
> Over the peaks of pride,
> Across the seas of mortal need,
> Its citizens abide.

> And through the distance though I see
> How stern must be the fare,
> My feet are ever fain to be
> Upon the journey there.
>
> In that far land the only school
> The dwellers all attend,
> Is built upon the Golden Rule.
> And man to man is friend.
>
> No war is there nor war's distress,
> But truth and love increase—
> It is a realm of pleasantness,
> And all her paths are peace.
>
> —*Leslie Pinckney Hill*

These stanzas are from four Negro poets whose voices have but lately been lifted in song—still living and youthful voices. To these I will add an utterance "from a voice that is still"—silenced in death, at the age of twenty-three years:

> THE MULATTO TO HIS CRITICS
>
> Ashamed of my race?
> And of what race am I?
> I am many in one.
> Of Red Man, Black Man, Briton, Celt, and Scot,
> Through my veins there flows the blood
> In warring clash and tumultuous riot.
> I welcome all,
> But love the blood of the kindly race
> That swarths my skin, crinkles my hair,
> And puts sweet music into my soul.
>
> —*Joseph S. Cotter, Jr.*

"Sweet music in the soul"—that is the Negro's boon from Heaven. The sweet music of the first stanza quoted in this essay came from the soul of the father of this Negro Lycidas. Verily, "We learn in suffering what we teach in song."

Poetry, in the popular mind, is no more than the fringe of a people's solid achievement, being merely decorative to railroads and factories, the products of mines and fields, big engineering feats and immense populations. Yet of ancient civilizations, not essentially inferior to our own, virtually all of moment that remains, or that passed into the world's sum of good, might be included under the term poetry; namely, the people's heroic deeds and heroic ideals and heroic dreams, embodied in some form of beauty—words, colors, or stone—all their material wealth, all that ministered merely to bodily comfort, or to vain pride, or to fleeting physical power, having perished and returned to that dust whence it sprung. This is the moral writ large in the ruins of a whole series of "mighty" empires. So outstanding a fact of history should induce reflection in the master spirits of our age, who seem not to have learned wisdom of Ninevah and Tyre, trite as they are as illustrations of the transitoriness and vanity of material wealth.

"Where there is no vision, the people perish." No vision; that is, no peering into the future for a truer and juster and lovlier order of things, no beholding afar off the ultimate goal of life, inspiring effort, battle, sacrifice, entailing sorrow, quickening joy, lifting up the soul in power. Vision, then, means all spiritual wealth, it means not merely religion in the restricted sense of that term, but that larger expression of the totality of life which we call poetry. Poetry is the witness of the vision, the embodiment of it. In its final analysis it is so much of a people's life as is not perishable. The Hebrew people in their great classic age— what did they, with their religious idealism, achieve but this? Their chronicles, their books of law, their books of wisdom, their prophecies—what are they, rightly conceived, but poems of a divine inspiration springing from great ethical purpose? Dreams, ideals, aspirations, and strivings, noble joys, and noble sorrows,— these are the substance of those sublime books. In modern times, in this Western World, we would call it all poetry. The difference of terminology must not be allowed to conceal from us an identity of character. For poetry through all the ages in the Western World has had the same austerity of purpose, the same unconquerableness of vision, the same sternness of rebuke for things as they are, the same yearning for things that should be, as prophecy had in the ancient oriental world.

Such is the dignity, the importance, of poetry. A people's poetry, therefore, affords the most serious subject of study to those who would understand that people—that people's soul, that people's status, that people's potentialities. A people that is producing poetry is not perishing, but is astir with life, with vital impulses, with life-giving visions. It is a people that is becoming noteworthy. Statesmen (or wanting these, politicians) may be warned to take notice. Employers of labor may be reminded, also, that there is a world of undreampt-of meaning in the old saying that man shall not live by bread alone. No men whatsoever live by bread alone.

Poetry, it may be said to a practical age, is the most practical thing in every age of the world, in every country whatsoever. It is really the most efficient thing, to use the watchword of our generation. It can build up, it can tear down, it can create revolutions. Nothing of human creation is more divine, more beneficent, more dangerous. As it is the friend of all noble aspiring, it is not less the foe of all that should not be, of custom that sins against justice, of tradition that wars against new-born truth, of all darkness that would extinguish the light, of all that is inhuman.

Less than a generation ago the announcement was made to an incredulous world that a Negro poet, a genuine black singer of genius, had appeared. A few white people, a very few, knew, vaguely, that back in Colonial times there was a slave woman in Boston who had written verses, who was therefore a prodigy. The space between Phillis Wheatley and this new singer was desert. But Nature produces freaks, or sports; therefore a Negro poet was not absolutely beyond belief, since poets are rather freakish, abnormal creatures anyway. Incredulity therefore yielded to an attitude scarcely worthier; namely, that dishonoring, irreverent interpretation of a supreme human phenomenon which consists in denominating it a freak of nature. The poet is Nature's sport, not God's gift. Dishonoring and irreverent both to humanity and to deity I call this skepticism.

But Dunbar is a fact, as Burns, as Whittier, as Riley, are facts—a fact of great moment to a people and for a people. But it is not of Dunbar I mean to speak here. He is known and accepted, in a manner. He needs no emphasis, though he does need interpretation. I mention Dunbar here only to draw attention to my theme, that theme being, not one poet, but a multitude animated by one spirit though characterized by diversity of talent, all spokesmen of their race in its new era. Dunbar does indeed appear to sustain a definite relation to these black singers of the new day. For one thing, he revealed to the Negro youth of our land the latent literary powers of their race, and, not less important, he revealed also the poetic materials at hand in the Negro people, lowly or distinguished. He may therefore be thought of as the fecundating genius of their muses. But I think they are born, as he was, of the creative Zeitgeist, sent of heaven.

But to give my assertion regarding Dunbar its proper significance, I must remark, for white people, that there were two Dunbars, and that they know but one. There is the Dunbar of " the jingle in a broken tongue," whom Howells with gracious but imperfect sympathy and understanding brought to the knowledge of the world, and whom the public readers, white and black alike (the sin is upon both), have found it delightful to present, to the entire eclipse of the other Dunbar. That other Dunbar was the poet of the flaming " Ode to Ethiopia," the pathetic lyric, " We Wear the Mask," and a score of other pieces in which, using their speech, he matches himself with the poets who shine as stars in the firmament of our admiration. This Dunbar, I say, Howells failed to appreciate, and ignorance of him has been fostered by professional readers and writers. The first Dunbar, the generally accepted one, was, as Howells pointed out, the artistic interpreter of the old-fashioned, vanishing generation of black folk—the generation that was maimed and scarred by slavery, that presented so many ludicrous and pathetic, abject and lovable aspects in strange mixture. The second Dunbar was the prophet robed in a mantle of austerity, shod with fire, bowed with sorrow, as every true prophet has been, in whatever time, among whatever people. He was the prophet, I say, of a new generation, a coming generation, as he was the poet of a vanishing generation. The generation of which he was the prophet-herald has arrived. Its most authentic representatives are the poets to whom I have referred.

There has been in these years a renaissance of the Negro soul, and poetry is one of its expressions. Other expressions there are and very significant ones, expressions which the world is taking note of since they are material or expressible in terms all men understand. Poetry is not of these. Yet poetry, I say, is perhaps the most potent and significant expression of the re-born soul of the Negro in this our day, in witness of which assertion this " prayer of the race that God made black " may be accepted:

> We would be peaceful, Father—but when we must,
> Help us to thunder hard the blow that's just.
> We would be manly, proving well our worth,
> Then would not cringe to any god on earth.
> We would be loving and forgiving, thus
> To love our neighbor as thou lovest us.
> We would be faithful, loyal to the Right,
> Ne'er doubting that the day will follow night.
> We would be all that Thou haṣt meant for man,
> Up through the ages, since the world began.
> God, save us in thy Heaven, where all is well!
> We come, slow-struggling, up the hills of Hell.

The author, Lucian B. Watkins, of Virginian birth, was wrecked in health in oversea's service, and died February 1, 1921, in the Fort McHenry Hospital, Maryland. From his sick bed he sent out poems of extraordinary merit and of great passion. Optimism is often said to be a characteristic of the Negro. Here are some stanzas from a poem entitled, "The Optimist," by Miss Ethyl Lewis:

> Never mind, children, be patient awhile,
> And carry your load with a nod and a smile,
> For out of the hell and the hard of it all,
> Time is sure to bring sweetest honey—not gall.
>
> Out of the hell and the hard of it all,
> A bright star shall rise that never shall fall:
> A God-fearing race—proud, noble, and true,
> Giving good for the evil which they always knew.
>
> * * * * *
>
> So dry your wet pillow and lift your bowed head
> And show to the world that hope is not dead!
> Be patient! Wait! See what yet may befall,
> Out of the hell and the hard of it all.

The Negro might well be expected to exhibit a gift for poetry. His gift for oratory has long been acknowledged. The fact has been accepted without reflection upon its significance. It should have been foreseen that because of the close kinship between oratory and poetry the Negro would some day, with more culture, achieve distinction in the latter art, as he had already achieved distinction in the former art. The endowments which make for distinction in these two great kindred arts, it must also be remarked, have not been properly esteemed in the Negro. In other races oratory and poetry have been accepted as the tokens of noble qualities of character, lofty spiritual gifts. Such they are, in all races. They spring from mankind's supreme spiritual impulses, from mankind's loftiest aspirations—the aspirations for freedom, for justice, for virtue, for honor and distinction.

That these impulses, these aspirations, and these endowments are in the American Negro and are now exhibiting themselves in verse,—it is this I wish to show to the skeptically minded. All will admit at once that the Negro nature is endowed above most others, if not all others, in fervor of feeling, in the completeness of self-surrender to emotion. Hence we see that marvelous display of rhythm in the individual and in the group. This capacity of submission to a higher harmony, a grander power, than self, affords the explanation of mankind's highest reaches of thought, supreme insights, and noblest expressions. Rhythm is its manifestation. It is the most central and compulsive law of the universe. The rhythmic soul falls into harmony and co-operation with the universal creative energy. It therefore becomes a creative soul.

But fervor of feeling must have some originating cause. That cause is an imagination—the vivid, concrete presentation of an object or idea to the mind. The Negro has this endowment also. Ideas enter his mind with a vividness and power which betoken an extraordinary faculty of imagination. The graphic originality of language commonly exhibited by the Negro would be sufficient proof of this were other proof wanting. And no one will deny to the Negro this gift. Whoever has listened to a colored preacher's sermon, either of the old or the new school, will recall perhaps more than one example of poetic phrasing, more than one word-picture, that rendered some idea vivid beyond vanishing. It no doubt has been made, in the ignorant or illiterate, an object of jest, just as the other two endowments have been; but these three gifts are the three supreme gifts of the poet, and the poet is the supreme outcome of the race. Power of feeling, power of imagination, power of expression,—these make the poet.

As a witness of the Negro's untutored gift for song there are the Spirituals, his "canticles of love and woe," chanted wildly, in that darkness which only a few rays from Heaven brightened. Since they afford, as it were, a background for the song of cultured art which now begins to appear, I must here give a word to these crude old plantation songs. They are one of the most notable contributions of any people, similarly circumstanced, to the world's treasury of song, altogether the most appealing. Their significance for history and for art—especially for art—awaits interpretation. There are signs that this interpretation is not far in the future. Dvorak, the Bohemian, aided by the Negro composer, Harry T. Burleigh, may have heralded, in his " New World Symphony," the consummate achievement of the future which shall be entirely the Negro's. Had Samuel Coleridge-Taylor been an American instead of an English Negro, this theme rather than the Indian theme might have occupied his genius.

But the sister art of poetry may anticipate music in the great feat of embodying artistically the yearning, suffering, prayerful soul of the African in those centuries when he could only with patience endure and trust in God—and wail these mournfullest of melodies. Some lyrical drama like " Prometheus Bound," but more touching as being more human; some epic like " Paradise Lost," but nearer to the common heart of man, and more lyrical; some " Divina Commedia " that shall be the voice of those silent centuries of slavery, as Dante's poem was the voice of the long-silent epoch preceding it, is the not improbable achievement of some descendant of the slaves.

In a poem of tender appeal, James Weldon Johnson has celebrated the " black and unknown bards," who, without art, and even without letters, produced from their hearts, weighed down with sorrows, the immortal Spirituals:

> O black and unknown bards of long ago,
> How came your lips to touch the sacred fire?
> How, in your darkness, did you come to know
> The power and beauty of the minstrel's lyre?
> Who first from midst his bonds lifted his eyes?
> Who first from out the still watch, lone and long,
> Feeling the ancient faith of prophets rise
> Within his dark-kept soul, burst into song?

So begins this noble tribute to the nameless natural poets from whose hearts, touched as a harp by the Divine Spirit, gave forth "Swing low, Sweet Chariot," and "Nobody Knows de Trouble I see," "Steal away to Jesus," and " Roll, Jordan, roll."

Great praise does indeed rightly belong to that black slave-folk who gave to the world this treasure of religious song. To the world, I say, for they belong as truly to the whole world as do the quaint and incomparable animal stories of Uncle Remus. Their appeal is to every human heart, but especially to the heart that has known great sorrow and which looks to God for help.

There is a book of rhymes which, every Christmas season, is the favorite gift, the most gladly received, of all that Santa Claus brings. Nor so at Christmas only ; it is a perennial pleasure, a boon to all children, young and old in years. This book is Mother Goose's Melodies. How many " immortal " epics of learned poets it has outlived! How many dainty volumes of polished lyrics has this humble book of " rhymes " seen vanish to the dusty realms of dark oblivion! In every home it has a place and is cherished. Its contents are better known and more loved than the contents of any other book. Untutored, nameless poets, nature-inspired, gave this priceless boon to all generations of children, and to all sorts and conditions—an immortal book if such there is.

As a life-long teacher and student of poetry, I venture, with no fear, the assertion that from no book of verse in our language can the whole art of poetry be so effectively learned as from " Mother Goose's Melodies." Every device of rhyme, and melody, and rhythm, and tonal color is exemplified here in a manner to produce the effects which all the great artists in verse aim at. This book that we all love—and patronize—is the greatest melodic triumph in our literature. And it is of unknown, though certainly humble, origin.

In the realm of sacred song the Negro Spirituals hold a like pre-eminence and have a like history. They are the Mother Goose's Melodies of sacred song. Out of such simple elements never were such effects produced. How meagre the vocabulary, how single the idea, what repetition! Yet how the impression is constantly deepened, how the emotion—which is the legitimate end of a song —is constantly intensified! They warm our hearts, as no other religious songs, to the melting point. They make our hearts glow with kindly feelings, with everlasting hopes, and with visions of eternal victory. This is religion on the emotional side. As thus ministering to our spiritual nature, these gifts of the spirit, these " Spirituals," are to be respected and held in reverence. I never wish to hear them, for my part, except from consecrated lips and reverential hearts.

In certain aspects these Spirituals suggest the songs of Zion, the Psalms. Trouble is the mother of song, particularly of religious song. In trouble the soul cries out to God—" a very present help in time of trouble." The Psalms and the Spirituals alike rise *de profundis*. But in one respect the songs of the African slaves differ from the songs of Israel in captivity: there is no prayer for vengeance in the Spirtuals, no vindictive spirit ever even suggested. We can but wonder now at this. For slavery at its best was unspeakably degrading, cruel, and oppressive. Yet no imprecation, such as mars so many a beautiful Psalm, ever found its way into a plantation Spiritual. A convincing testimony this to that spirit in the African slave which Christ, by precept and example, sought to establish in his disciples. If the Negro in our present day is growing bitter toward the white race, does it not behoove us to inquire why it is so, in view of his indisputable patience, meekness, and good-nature? We might find in our present regime a more intolerable cruelty than belonged even to slavery, if we investigated honestly. There is certainly a bitter and vindictive tone in much of the Afro-American verse now appearing in the colored press. Alas, that it is so. For both races it augurs ill.

In a very striking way these folk-songs of the plantation suggest the old English folk-songs of unknown authorship and origin —the ancient traditional ballads, long despised and neglected, but ever living on and loved in the hearts of the people. This unstudied poetry of the people, the unlettered common folk, had supreme virtues, the elemental and universal virtues of simplicity, sincerity, veracity. It had the power, in an artificial age, to bring poetry back to reality, to genuine emotion, to effectiveness, to the common interests of mankind. Simple and crude as it was it had a merit unknown to the polished verse of the schools. Potential Negro poets might do well to ponder this fact of literary history. There is nothing more precious in English literature than this crude old poetry of the people.

But I have not yet indicated the precise place of these Spirituals in the world's treasury of song. Their closest kinship is with—not " Mother Goose's Melodies," not the old English ballads, nor yet the Psalms of Israel—but the song offerings, the chanted prayers, of the primitive Church, of the Church in the age of persecution, the litanies

> "—that came
> Like the volcano's tongue of flame
> Up from the burning core below—
> The canticles of love and woe."

These songs might be called the melodious tears of slaves. An African proverb says, "We weep in our hearts like the tortoise." *In their hearts*—so wept the slaves, silently save for these mournful cries in melody. Without means of defense, save a nature armored with faith, when assailed, insulted, oppressed, they could but imitate the tortoise when he shuts himself up in his shell and patiently takes the blows that fall. The world knew not then, nor fully knows now—partly because of African buoyancy, pliability, and optimism—what tears they wept. These Spirituals are the golden vials spoken of in Holy Writ, "full of odors, which are the prayers of saints"—an everlasting memorial before the throne of God. Other vials there are, the vials of wrath, and these, too, are at God's right hand.

A Negro sculptor, Mrs. Meta Warrick Fuller, not knowing of this proverb about the tortoise which has only recently been brought from Africa, but simply interpreting Negro life in America, has embodied the very idea of the African saying in bronze. Under the title "Secret Sorrow" a man is represented as eating his own heart.

The interpretation in art of the Spirituals, or a poetry of art developed along the lines and in the spirit of those songs, is something we may expect the black singers of no distant day to produce. Already we have many a poem that offers striking reminiscences or traits of the Spirituals.

The Negro singer of this era, the heir of those "black and unknown bards," has indeed a noble heritage of song. And if there is any shame (which there is) the shame is not the Negro's; but the glory is. Therefore, let him sing triumphantly the old song, and add to it a new one, like, but with other elements of power from a higher art.

Two or three poems will make clearer my meaning with reference to the kinship of some of the best Negro verse of the present day with the Spirituals.

THE BAND OF GIDEON

The band of Gideon roam the sky,
The howling wind is their war-cry,
The thunder's roll is their trumpet's peal,
And the lightnings flash their vengeful steel.
    Each black cloud
    Is a fiery steed.
    And they cry aloud
    With each strong deed,
" The Sword of the Lord and Gideon."

And men below rear temples high
And mock their God with reasons why,
And live in arrogance, sin, and shame,
And rape their souls for the world's good name.
    Each black cloud
    Is a fiery steed.
    And they cry aloud
    With each strong deed,
" The Sword of the Lord and Gideon."

The band of Gideon roam the sky
And view the earth with baleful eye;
In holy wrath theey scourge the land
With earthquake, storm, and burning brand.
    Each black cloud
    Is a fiery steed.
    And they cry aloud
    With each strong deed,
" The Sword of the Lord and Gideon."

'The lightnings flash and the thunders roll,
And " Lord have mercy on my soul,"
Cry men as they fall on the stricken sod,
In agony searching for their God.
    Each black cloud
    Is a fiery steed.
    And they cry aloud
    With each strong deed,
" The Sword of the Lord and Gideon."

And men repent and then forget
That heavenly wrath they ever met.
The band of Gideon yet will come
And strike their tongues of blasphemy dumb.
    Each black cloud
    Is a fiery steed.
    And they cry aloud
    With each strong deed,
" The Sword of the Lord and Gideon."
                                    —*Joseph S. Cotter, Jr.*

    The reader, I predict, will be drawn back again and again to this mysteriously powerful poem. It will continue to haunt his imagination. The stamp of genius, African genius, is upon it. Closely allied, on the one hand, by its august refrain, to the

Spirituals, on the other hand it touches the most refined and perfected art; such, for example, as Rossetti's ballads or Vachel Lindsay's cantatas. The author at his early death, in 1918, left behind a thin volume of lyrics, a little book of one-act plays, and an unfinished sonnet sequence of extraordinary beauty.[1] Joseph S. Cotter, Sr., the father, is still living, in Louisville, Kentucky. He is a playwright, fabulist, poet, and schoolmaster. His great variety and range even as a poet alone cannot be represented here, but the following sonnet will reveal that we have in Cotter a poet of no common sort.

THE PROPHET

He saw life masquerade in Babylon,
   He saw Life jaded by the mystic Nile,
While weaving tapestry of brick and stone
   To mesh its merriment and seal its smile.
He brought the fore-time to this after-time,
   He questioned workers, warriors, poets, sages,
Then whispered to himself: " Nor tribe, nor clime,
   Nor God, nor Devil can unwed the ages."
The Prophet felt the ache that we are feeling,
   The Prophet saw the greed that bows us under;
And heard the echo of our tense appealing
   For brotherhood that dares not halt nor blunder.
The Past will be the Present. Let us make
To-day tomorrow for our children's sake.

To this, also, I predict, the reader will return for more than one perusal and then its idea will remain in his thoughts.

To Mrs. Alice Dunbar-Nelson, the widow of the poet Dunbar, we are indebted for one of the most beautiful sonnets ever written.

I had not thought of violets of late,
   The wild, shy kind that spring beneath your feet
In wistful April days, when lovers mate
   And wander through the fields in raptures sweet.
The thoughts of violets meant florists' shops,
   And bows and pins, and perfumed papers fine;
And garish lights, and mincing little fops,
   And cabarets and songs, and deadening wine.
So far from sweet real things my thoughts had strayed,
   I had forgot wide fields and clear brown streams;
The perfect loveliness that God has made—
   Wild violets shy and Heaven-mounting dreams.
And now—unwittingly, you've made me dream
Of violets, and my soul's forgotten gleam.

---

[1] Published in the *A. M. E. Zion Quarterly Review* (New York), XXXI, 3

Elizabeth Barrett Browning or Christina Rossetti could have placed her signature to that sonnet without danger to her fame. A passion for nature is one of the traits of the true poet. In several of the Negro poets of to-day I find this passion gaining artistic expression. From Charles Bertram Johnson's "Songs of My People" I take the following exquisite lyric:

A RAIN SONG

Chill the rain falls, chill!
Dull gray the world ; the vale
Rain-swept; wind-swept the hill;
"But gloom and doubt prevail,"
My heart breaks forth to say.

Ere thus its sorrow note,
"Cheer up! Cheer up! to-day,
To-morrow is to be,"
Babbled from a joyous throat,
A robin's, in a mist-gray tree.

Then off to keep a tryst-
He preened his drabbled cloak—
Doughty little optimist!
As if in answer, broke
The sunlight thru that oak.

Mr. Johnson, whose home is Moberly, Missouri, is schoolmaster, preacher, and, I think you will agree, poet. The following stanza-poem—he affords many such—both represents his artistry and is a poignantly pathetic comment upon a little understood race:

MY PEOPLE

My people laugh and sing
 And dance to death—
None imagining
 The heartbreak under breath.

Death and the mysteries of life, the pain and the grief that flesh and soul are heirs to, the eternal problems that address themselves to all generations and races, produce in the soul of the Negro the same reactions as of old they produced in the soul of David or of Homer, or as, in our own day, in the soul of a Wordsworth or a Shelley. Of this we have a glimpse in the following lyric, from Mr. Walter Everette Hawkins:

IN SPITE OF DEATH

Curses come in every sound,
And wars spread gloom and woe around.
The cannon belch forth death and doom,
But still the lilies wave and bloom.
Man fills the earth with grief and wrong,
But cannot hush the bluebird's song.
My stars are dancing on the sea,
The waves fling kisses up at me.
Each night my gladsome moon doth rise ;
A rainbow spans my evening skies ;
The robin's song is full and fine;
And roses lift their lips to mine.

The jonquils ope their petals sweet,
The poppies dance around my feet;
In spite of winter and of death,
The Spring is in the zephyr's breath.

The kinship of souls, a truth which all of this poetry impresses upon the reader, finds explicit expression in the following lines from Mr. Leon R. Harris:

We travel a common road, Brother,—
We walk and we talk much the same ;
We breathe the same sweet air of heaven—
Strive alike for fortune and fame;
We laugh when our hearts fill with gladness,
We weep when we're smothered in woe;
We strive, we endure, we seek wisdom;
We sin—and we reap what we sow.
Yes, all who would know it can see that
When everything's put to the test,
In spite of our color and features,
The Negro's the same as the rest.

In the poetry which the Negro is producing to-day there is a challenge to the world. His race has been deeply stirred by recent events; its reaction has been mighty. The challenge, spoken by one, but for the race, the inarticulate millions as well as the cultured few, comes thus:

TO AMERICA

How would you have us—as we are,
  Or sinking 'neath the load we bear?
Our eyes fixed forward on a star?
  Or gazing empty at despair?
Rising or falling? Men or things?
  With dragging pace, or footsteps fleet?
Strong, willing, sinews in your wings?
  Or tightening chains about your feet?
                    —*James Weldon Johnson*

The World War, in which the Negroes gave liberally, patriotically, heroically, of their blood and treasure for democracy, quickened dying hopes and begot new aspirations in them—hopes and aspirations the absence of which would rank them lower in the scale of humanity. Out of many poetic expressions of this reaction I choose the following, from " The Heart of the World and Other Poems," by Joshua Henry Jones, Jr.:

THE HEART OF THE WORLD

In the heart of the world is the call for peace—
    Up-surging, symphonic roar.
'Tis ill of all clashings ; it seeks release
    From fetters of greed and gore.
The winds of the battlefields echo the sigh
    Of heroes slumbering deep,
Who gave all they had and now dreamlessly lie
    Where the bayonets sent them to sleep.
    Peace for the wealthy ; peace for the poor ;
    Peace on the hillside, and peace on the moor.

In the heart of the world is the call for love :
    For fingers to bind up the wound,
Slashed deep by the ruthless, harsh hand of might,
    When Justice is crushed to the ground.
'Tis ill of the fevers of fear of the strong—
    Of jealousies—prejudice—pride.
" Is there no ideal that's proof against wrong?
    Man asks of the man at his side.
    Right for the lowly ; right for the great ;
    Right all to pilot to happiness' gate.

In the heart of the world is the call for love:
    White heart—Red—Yellow—and Black.
Each face turns to Bethlehem's bright star above,
    Though wolves of self howl at each back.
The whole earth is lifting its voice in a prayer
    That nations may learn to endure,
Without killing and maiming, but doing what's fair
    With a soul that is noble and pure.
    Love in weak peoples ; love in the strong ;
    Love that will banish all hatred and wrong.

In the heart of the world is the call of God ;
    East—West—and North—and South.
Stirring, deep-yearning, breast-heaving call for God
    A-tremble behind each mouth.
The heart's ill of torments that rend men's souls.
    Skyward lift all faiths and hopes ;
Across all the oceans the evidence rolls,
    Refreshing all life's arid slopes.
    God in the highborn ; God in the low ;
    God calls us, world-brothers. Hark ye! and know.

There is not in all our poetic literature a more eloquent apostrophe to our country's flag than I am able to offer here from a Negro poet. The writer, Edward Smyth Jones, is author of a volume entitled *The Sylvan Cabin.*

FLAG OF THE FREE

Flag of the free, our sable sires
   First bore thee long ago
Into hot battles' hell-lit fires,
   Against the fiercest foe.
And when he shook his shaggy mien,
   And made the death-knell ring,
Brave Attucks fell upon the Green,
   Thy stripes first crimsoning!

Thy might and majesty we hurl,
   Against the bolts of Mars ;
And from thy ample folds unfurl
   Thy field of flaming stars!
Fond hope to nations in distress,
   Thy starry gleam shall give;
The stricken in the wilderness
   Shall look to thee and live.

What matter if where Boreas roars,
   Or where sweet Zephyr smiles?
What matter it where eagle soars,
   Or in the sunlit isles ;
The flowing crimson stripes shall wave
   Above the bluish brine,
Emblazoned ensign of the brave,
   And Liberty enshrine!

Flag of the Free, still float on high
   Through every age to come ;
Bright beacon of the azure sky,
   True light of Freedom's dome.
Till nations all shall cease to grope
   In vain for liberty,
O shine, last lingering star of hope
   Of all humanity!

It has often been disputed that didacticism is consistent with poetry. But is there not always a didactic power in "noble ideas nobly expressed," which poetry is? To the credit of its writers much of the best Negro verse of the times is didactic. Wordsworth said he had learned from Burns, who walked in glory following his plow,

"How verse may build a princely throne
On humble truth."

when didacticism can be infused with emotion, emotion akin to religious feeling, and made to delight by the witchery of art, we may welcome it and rejoice in it. Beauty and Use have then joined in wedlock. Two poems of this character I will present. The first is from a schoolmaster whom I have already introduced —Joseph S. Cotter, Sr.:

THE NEGRO CHILD

My little one of ebon hue,
  My little one with fluffy hair,
The wide, wide world is calling you
  To think and do and dare.

The lessons of stern yesterdays
  That stir your blood and poise your brain
Are etching out the simple ways
  By which you must attain.

An echo here, a memory there,
  An act that links itself with truth ;
A vision that makes troubles air
  And toils the joy of youth:

These be your food, your drink, your rest,
  These be your moods of drudgeful ease,
For these be nature's spur and test
  And heaven's fair degrees.

My little one of ebon hue,
  My little one with fluffy hair,
Go train your head and hands to do,
  Your head and heart to dare.

The one following is from a sixteen-year-old school girl, Miss Elna Ardell Woods, tenth grade, Hattiesburg, Mississippi:

MAKE A SUCCESS OF YOURSELF

Make a success of yourself,
  Don't worry too much about fame.
Or power in the struggle for pelf,
  Just make a success of your name.
Be one that is rated at par
  In the markets of men every day,
Be all that good fellows are,
  Don't live in a slovenly way.

Make yourself live as you should,
  Make yourself carry a smile,
Be sure that your character's good,
  Be sure that your word is worth while ;
Play fair though you win or you lose,
  Be kindly and true to the end,
Be the same sort of man that you'd choose
  To have as a comrade and friend.

> The battle of life's not so hard
> If only you'll fight as a man ;
> There are many to stand by and guard
> And help you as much as they can,
> But it's you that you offer for sale,
> With your traits ranged like goods on a shelf,
> And the first thing to do without fail,
> Is to make a success of yourself.

It is no matter for surprise, in view of the great strides the Negroes of our land have made in the acquisition of property and education, and in advancing themselves every way, that their poets should celebrate their achievements. Leon R. Harris thus writes of the progress of his people:

> We've builded our schools and our churches
> By paths where our slave fathers trod;
> We've trained our hands for a living,
> Our minds and our hearts to see God.
> We've laughed at our trials and troubles,
> Our confidence quenching our fears ;
> We've sung away sorrow and sadness:
> We've prayed away poverty's tears.

Mr. Harris, now editor of *The Richmond Blade* (Indiana) was reared in an orphanage, had a few terms in the common schools, obtained by his own efforts two years at Berea and three years at Tuskegee, and was until a year or so ago a worker in a furnace factory. A poem of his entitled "The Steel Makers" is remarkable for its intrinsic merit, for its glorification of work, and for its interpretation of the life of his fellow-workmen. I will give the opening lines:

> Filled with the vigor such jobs demand,
> Strong of muscle and steady of hand,
> Before the flaming furnaces stand
>   The men who make the steel.
> Midst the sudden sounds of falling bars,
> Midst the clang and bang of cranes and cars,
> Where the earth beneath them jerks and jars,
>   They work with willing zeal.
>
> They meet each task as they meet each day,
> Ready to labor and full of play ;
> Their faces are grimy, their hearts are gay,
>   There is sense in the songs they sing ;
> While stooped like priests at the holy mass,
> In the beaming light of the lurid gas,
> Their jet-black shadows each other pass,
>   And their hammers loudly ring.

> What do they see through the furnace door,
> From which the dazzling white lights pour?
> Ah, more than the sizzling liquid ore
> They see as they gaze within!

The rest of the poem pictures the visions of the workers—visions of all the future shapes and uses of the steel they are making. These verses place you in imagination amid the sights and sounds described, and they have something of the quality of steel bars.

It is manifestly impossible, in a pamphlet like this, to cover the entire range of contemporary Negro verse or to represent the work of all writers worthy of representation. In twice this number of pages it might be done. I seek here mainly to direct attention to this work, not to satisfy interest. A number of the best singers of the day have of necessity been omitted.

If one meets here but with the rhymes and rhythms and forms, as he may think, which are familiar to him in the poetry of the white race, let him reflect that only in that poetry has the Negro had an opportunity to be educated. He has been educated away from his own heritage and his own endowments. The Negro's native wisdom should lead him back to his natural founts of song. Our educational system should allow of and provide for this. His own literature in his schools is a reasonable policy.

As regards the essential significance of this poetry, one of its makers, Miss Eva A. Jessye, has said in a beautiful way almost what I wish to say. Her poem shall therefore conclude this presentation:

THE SINGER

> Because his speech was blunt and manner plain
> Untaught in subtle phrases of the wise,
> Because the years of slavery and pain
> Ne'er dimmed the light of faith within his eyes ;
> Because of ebon skin and humble pride,
> The world with hatred thrust the youth aside.
>
> But fragrance wafts from every trodden flower,
> And through our grief we rise to nobler things,
> Within the heart in sorrow's darkest hour
> A well of sweetness there unbidden springs ;
> Despised of men, discarded and alone—
> The world of nature claimed him as her own.

She taught him truths that liberate the soul
From bonds more galling than the slaver's chain—
That manly natures, lily-wise, unfold
Amid the mire of hatred void of stain ;
Thus in his manhood, clean, superbly strong,
To him was born the priceless gift of song.

The glory of the sun, the hush of morn,
Whisperings of tree-top faintly stirred,
The desert silence, wilderness forlorn,
Far ocean depths, the tender lilt of bird ;
Of hope, despair, he sang, his melody
The endless theme of life's brief symphony.

And nations marvelled at the minstrel lad,
Who swayed emotions as his fancy led ;
With him they wept, were melancholy, sad ;
" 'Tis but a cunning jest of Fate," they said ;
They did not dream in selfish sphere apart
That song is but the essence of the heart.